The American Revolutionary War & The Birth Of A Nation Trivia

Test Your Knowledge On The Cause Of The War, The Founding Fathers, The Declaration of Independence, and What Was Happening In Our Nation During These Trying Times

Cheryl Pryor

Arlington & Amelia

ISBN-13:978-1886541146

ISBN-10:1886541140

FOR

SKIP, HOLLY, AND CHELSEY

TABLE OF CONTENTS

Other Books by Cheryl Pryor

Legacy

Write Now!

Wedding Survival Guide

The Big Book of Presidential Trivia

The Big Book of First Ladies Trivia

Children's Books

Trivia For Kids Series

The Presidents

The First Ladies

The Sullivan Family Series

Savannah's Big Move

Savannah On Stage

Savannah On Horseback

Savannah In Look What Followed Me Home

Savannah and the Grumpy Neighbor

Savannah and the Mad Scientist

Savannah's World Travel Series

Savannah's Disney World Celebration

Savannah Goes To Paris

1

TEST YOUR KNOWLEDGE

Answers are given at the end of the chapter.

1. What was one of the fears the men of the Continental Congress were concerned about in declaring a fight for independence?

2. Which event occurred first: The Boston Massacre or The Boston Tea Party?

3. Where did 'the shot heard 'round the world' take place?

4. Who fired the first shot: the British or the colonials?

5. **True or False.** At the beginning of the war, the colonists were fighting for their independence.

6. Who wrote *'Common Sense,'* a pamphlet arguing for independence?

7. Who was King of England during the Revolutionary War?

8. Who was Commander-in-Chief during the Revolutionary War?

9. Who was the most famous traitor of the American cause during the Revolutionary War?

10. What city was known as the Tory capital of America?

11. Who were the Loyalists?

12. This nation was formed out of how many colonies?

13. What was the purpose of the liberty pole in the days leading up to the Revolutionary War?

14. What was a minuteman?

15. **True or False.** Making military preparations before the beginning of the Revolutionary War, with no means of making weapons, the patriots began raiding armories.

16. What year was the official birth of the U.S. Navy?

17. During the days of the American Revolutionary War, and before, what was the quickest way to travel from one colony to another?

18. How many colonies went to war with the British in the Revolutionary War?

19. Where were the headquarters, or capital, of the colonies during the Revolutionary War?

20. Who wrote the famous poem *'The Midnight Ride'* which made many people aware for the first time who Paul Revere was?

21. What was the color of the uniform of the Continental army?

22. What was the color of the uniform of the British army?

23. What disease had spread through Washington's army?

24. In what state was Valley Forge, Washington's winter headquarters located?

25. In what way did France's part in the Revolutionary War lead to the outbreak of the French Revolution?

26. Other than France, what other countries joined to fight for the American cause?

27. What treaty ended the American Revolutionary War?

28. On the night of Dec. 16, 1773, men disguised themselves as Mohawk Indians and boarded three ships in Boston Harbor. They dumped 342 cases of tea overboard. This act has gone down in history known as what?

Answers - Chapter 1

Test Your Knowledge

1. *Any of the answers below would be correct*

a) Britain was the strongest military power in the world

b) Would the colonists be able to fight the British with limited supplies; they were concerned that when it was discovered the colonists wanted their independence Britain would not accede willingly

c) Would the colonies be so weak at the end of the war that the French or Spanish would come in and overtake them

2. Boston Massacre

3. Lexington (Massachusetts) in what became known as The Battle of Concord

4. No one really knows which side fired the first shot.

5. False

It wasn't until early in 1776 that Congress voted for independence.

6. Thomas Paine

7. George III

8. George Washington

9. Benedict Arnold

10. New York City

11. People who did not want to fight against the British but remained loyal to the king were known as Loyalists.

12. 13

13. A red banner would be flown from the pole to call a meeting.

14. Militia ready to meet and fight at a minute's notice.

15. True.

They also began purchasing gun powder and arms from France and the Netherlands.

16. 1775

17. By sea

18. 13

19. Philadelphia

20. Henry Wadsworth Longfellow

21. If you said either brown or blue you would be correct.

* *Congress initially stated the uniform should be brown, but with a shortage of supplies when shipments of blue coats arrived from France they switched to blue.*

22. Red

Which is why the British were also known as the Redcoats.

23. Smallpox

Typhoid or dysentery are also correct; though smallpox was the biggest concern.

24. Pennsylvania

25. France's national debt soared after aiding America, quadrupling France's debt which made the king look for new sources of revenue at home to a people who were already starving and suffering. Besides, the example of America having no king looked pretty good to the people of France.

26. Spain and the Netherlands

Spain did not consider themselves allies with the Americans nor did they recognize the United States or establish diplomatic relations until the end of the war. They gave the Americans some money, but that was as far as they were willing to participate. The Dutch sold us arms and munitions.

27. Treaty of Paris

28. The Boston Tea Party

2

WHAT LED TO THE AMERICAN REVOLUTIONARY WAR

Answers are given at the end of the chapter.

1. What started the French and Indian War? *(No, I'm not getting my wars mixed up.)*

2. The British national debt was staggering after funding the French and Indian War. For the first time, British Parliament passed a tax which would raise money from the colonists. What Act was passed to increase duties on products the colonists purchased?

3. What action did the colonists take when learning the British planned to put into action taxing goods they purchased?

4. The Proclamation of 1763, meant to appease the Native

Americans by assuring them the settlers wouldn't expand their lands west of the Appalachian Divide, angered the colonists. What were the settlers opposed to?

5. The British kept a large force in the colonies which the colonists took as a sign of the British suppressing their freedoms. The colonists were further outraged when the British implemented the Quartering Act of 1765. How did this Act affect the colonists?

6. The Stamp Act was passed in 1765 which affected the colonists in a way no other Act previously had, and they had no say in the matter. By boycotting British goods, was this effective in putting an end to the Stamp Act?

7. Parliaments passed laws increasing tax on items including tea. The colonists thinking the problem had been resolved with the repeal of The Stamp Act were angry. Name one of the ways the colonists responded.

8. What happened at the event that became known throughout history as the Boston Massacre?

9. What happened to the British soldiers of the Boston Massacre?

10. What well-known colonist and patriot, who was an attorney, defended the British soldiers from the Boston Massacre?

11. What British General arrived in Boston, along with four thousand troops, to take over as Governor of Massachusetts?

12. General Gage planned to raid the munitions depot in Concord and to capture two Patriot leaders. Who were the Patriot leaders he wanted to capture?

Answers – Chapter 2

What Led To The American Revolutionary War

Answers are given at the end of the chapter.

1. The French and Indian War was started over British concerns of French expansion in the Ohio valley.

2. The Sugar Act

* The colonists had become accustomed to governing themselves by this point, and felt the Sugar Act taxed the colonists in a way they felt only their own elected representatives should have the power to do.

3. The colonists planned to boycott imported British goods.

4. They felt by expanding westward would allow them the opportunity to purchase cheap land to farm and expand. They didn't want to be limited on where they could live.

5. The Quartering Act required the colonists to house and feed the

British troops.

6. Yes.

It hurt British merchants who relied on selling their goods to the colonies. The British Parliament repealed the Stamp Act and cut back on the provisions of the Sugar Act.

7. *Any of these answers would be correct.*

a) Boycott

b) Sons of Liberty were formed

c) Mobs formed

d) Seizures of ships

e) Attacking British commissioners

f) The sacking of their homes.

8. It started as a snowball fight that Crispus Attucks, an African American, and a group of men and boys used against a sentry guarding the State House. It ended when British troops came to reinforce the sentry and were frightened by the mob and fired into the crowd killing Crispus Attucks, and four others, and wounding half a dozen others.

9. They were charged with murder.

10. John Adams

He believed everyone deserved a fair trial even though his decision to defend the British troops angered many.

11. General Thomas Gage

12. Samuel Adams and John Hancock

3

BOSTON TEA PARTY

Answers are given at the end of the chapter.

1. Who was the leader of the Boston Tea Party?

2. How did the Patriots disguise themselves during the Boston Tea Party?

3. What year did the Boston Tea Party take place?

4. During the Boston Tea Party, what were the colonists protesting?

5. How much tea was dumped in the harbor during the Boston Tea Party?

6. Why did the participants of the Boston Tea Party dress up as Native Americans?

7. Most of the participants of the Boston Tea Party are names most Americans wouldn't recognize as they were everyday people who believed strongly in their cause. However, there are two names that all Americans should recognize that participated. Can you name one of them?

8. After the Boston Tea Party, the British government passed the Coercive Acts, which were a series of four acts meant to restore order and punish the colonists for their actions. What did the colonists call these Acts?

Answers – Chapter 3

Boston Tea Party

1. Samuel Adams

2. Native Americans

3. 1773

4. Taxation

5. Approximately 45 tons

6. Destroying the tea was an act of treason, so the colonists were disguising their identities.

7. Paul Revere or Sam Adams

8. The Intolerable Acts

4

FOUNDING FATHERS

Answers are given at the end of the chapter.

1. America's Founding Fathers structured America's democracy. How many of the Founding Fathers can you name?

2. Which Founding Father became Commander-in-Chief during the Revolutionary War?

3. Which Founding Father, who would later become one of our presidents, served under General George Washington during the Revolutionary War?

4. Which Founding Father drafted a Statute of Religious Liberty in 1786, which is a statement of both freedom of conscience and the principle of separation of church and state?

5. Which Founding Father was sent by Congress to France as an American diplomat to help secure aid for the American cause?

6. Which is the only Founding Father to have signed all four of the key documents that established the United States: the Declaration of Independence in 1776, the Treaty of Alliance with France in 1778, the Treaty of Paris in 1783, and the Constitution in 1787?

7. Which Founding Father became our nation's first president?

8. How many Founding Fathers became presidents of the United States? Can you name them?

9. Which Founding Father is most remembered by the way he signed the Declaration of Independence?

10. Which Founding Father was fatally shot in a duel by Aaron Burr?

Answers – Chapter 4

Founding Fathers

1. George Washington, John Adams, Thomas Jefferson, James Madison, James Monroe, Alexander Hamilton, Ben Franklin are the main ones that come to mind; but you can also add Patrick Henry, Samuel Adams, Thomas Paine, and members of the Constitutional Convention to the list.

2. George Washington

3. James Monroe

4. Thomas Jefferson

5. Benjamin Franklin

6. Benjamin Franklin

7. George Washington

8. 5. The first five presidents were all Founding Fathers.
They are: George Washington, John Adams, Thomas Jefferson,

James Madison, and James Monroe.

9. John Hancock

10. Alexander Hamilton

5

CONTINENTAL CONGRESS

Answers are given at the end of the chapter.

1. Delegates from every colony but one met in Philadelphia arrived for the First Continental Congress. Which colony was not represented?

2. **True or False.** Previous to the meeting of the First Continental Congress, colonists recognized themselves as from the state where they lived, such as 'I am a Virginian.' They now came together and thought of themselves as Americans for the first time.

3. **True or False.** The First Continental Congress initially met the demands of the British.

4. Americans sent an Olive Branch Petition to the British king along with a document declaring their reasons for having taken up arms. Did the king accept the petition?

5. A Continental army was needed once the King rejected the Americans Olive Branch Petition. Who did John Adams promote to be the Commander-in-Chief?

6. **True or False.** On July 2, 1776 when the states voted for

independence, the vote was unanimous for independence.

7. Who was the only member of Congress to actually sign the Declaration of Independence on July 4th?

8. What two brothers from Virginia signed the Declaration of Independence?

9. Who was the only man to sign the Articles of Association, the Declaration of Independence, the Articles of Confederation, and the Constitution?

10. What purpose did the Articles of Confederation serve?

11. Who drafted the Articles of Confederation?

12. What purpose did the Articles of Confederation, which were desperately needed during wartime, serve?

13. Where was the First Continental Congress held?

14. **True or False.** Some members of Congress, including John Adams, had contemplated replacing Washington as Commander-in-Chief.

Answers – Chapter 5

Continental Congress

1. Georgia

2. True

3. False

* *They sent demands to the king.*

4. He rejected both the Olive Branch Petition and their reasons for taking up arms.

5. George Washington

6. True

7. John Hancock, the President of the Continental Congress.

8. Richard Henry Lee and Francis Lightfoot Lee

9. Roger Sherman

10. It served as the United States first Constitution.

11. John Dickinson

12. *Any of the answers below would be correct.*

a) States remained sovereign and independent.

b) Congress was to serve as a last resort to settle a dispute.

c) Congress now had the authority to make treaties and alliances.

d) Maintain armed forces.

e) Make money – which was a necessity during wartime.

13. Philadelphia

14. True

* *It may have been discussed, but it was never proposed.*

6

THE DECLARATION OF INDEPENDENCE

Answers are given at the end of the chapter.

1. How many members were on the committee to write the Declaration of Independence?

2. Who wrote the Declaration of Independence?

3. Five men were selected to draft a declaration for independence. How many of these men can you name?

4. Complete this line from the Declaration of Independence: *'We hold these truths to be self-evident, that all men are created _____, that they are endowed by their _____ with certain unalienable Rights; that among these are _____, _____, and the pursuit of _____.*

5. Whose words did Thomas Jefferson receive inspiration from when writing the Declaration of Independence?

6. How long did it take Thomas Jefferson to write the Declaration of Independence?

7. In what state did Thomas Jefferson write the Declaration of Independence?

8. What is written on the back of the original copy of the Declaration of Independence?

9. How many men signed the Declaration of Independence?

10. **True or False.** Everyone who signed the Declaration of Independence was born in the United States.

11. Who was the first person to sign the Declaration of Independence?

12. Who was the oldest person who signed the Declaration of Independence?

13. Most of the men were in their forties and fifties when they signed the Declaration of Independence. Ben Franklin was the oldest at age seventy when he signed the document. Who was the youngest signer at age twenty-six?

14. Which signer of the Declaration of Independence was the first to propose a resolution to the Continental Congress stating that the colonies should be independent of Britain?

15. Of all the colonies, which one had the most signatures?

16. Why didn't John Dickinson sign the Declaration of Independence?

17. Once the Declaration of Independence had been written, approved, and signed, two hundred copies were made which were to be distributed throughout the colonies. What are the copies called?

18. What date was independence formally declared?

19. How many surviving Dunlap Broadsides are known to be in existence today?

20. Which two people who signed the Declaration of Independence went on to become president of the United States?

21. Other than John Hancock, what month did the other men sign the Declaration of Independence?

22. Where was the first public reading of the Declaration of Independence?

23. One man in Congress had opposed the resolution for independence. He wasn't willing to sign the Declaration of Independence and resigned from Congress. Who was he?

24. Did Samuel Adams sign the Declaration of Independence?

25. Who signed not only the Declaration of Independence, but also the Constitution?

26. How many men that signed the Declaration of Independence were dead before the end of the Revolutionary War?

27. Which man who signed the Declaration of Independence was the only signer to live long enough to celebrate the 50th anniversary of the signing of this document?

Answers – Chapter 6

The Declaration of Independence

1. 5

2. Thomas Jefferson

3. Thomas Jefferson, John Adams, Benjamin Franklin, Roger Sherman, and Robert Livingston

4. equal – creator - life, liberty, happiness

5. John Locke

6. 17 days

7. Pennsylvania

8. Original Declaration of Independence / dated July 4, 1776

According to the National Archives they assume the document was rolled up for storage and the notation was a label.

9. 56

10. False

* *The United States didn't exist until after the Declaration of Independence was signed.*

11. John Hancock

12. Ben Franklin

13. Edward Rutledge

* *Thomas Lynch, Jr. was also 26 years old.*

14. Richard Henry Lee

15. Pennsylvania

16. He was hoping for a reconciliation with the British.

17. Dunlap Broadsides

* *They were called this after the printer, John Dunlap, who printed them for distribution.*

18. July 2, 1776

19. 26

20. John Adams and Thomas Jefferson

21. August

22. Independence Hall

23. John Dickinson

24. Yes

25. Roger Sherman

26. 9

27. Charles Carroll from Maryland

7

BATTLES OF THE REVOLUTIONARY WAR

Answers are given at the end of the chapter.

1. Where were the first shots fired of the Revolutionary War?

2. The Battle of Lexington was a small fight. What was it's significance?

3. In what city was the Battle of Bunker Hill?

4. Who led the Colonial troops at the Battle of Bunker Hill?

5. Americans fired into the British at what is known as The Battle of Bunker Hill, even though most of the fighting took place on Breed's Hill, until the British had to retreat several times. Who won this battle?

6. Where did the first major battle fought by George Washington and the Continental army take place?

7. What battle was the turning point of the Revolutionary War?

8. What American victory convinced the French to recognize the patriot's cause and lend aid to them in the war?

9. With what country did the colonies alliance with which changed the War of Independence into a global fight?

10. What major issue was Shay's Rebellion over?

11. What city did the Americans receive their worst defeat of the war?

12. **True or False.** The battle off Chesapeake Bay, was a naval battle that made a large impact on world history.

13. What is the name of the battle that is one of the more historically known battles that took place after General George Washington and his troops crossed the Delaware River on Christmas night surprising the Hessians the next morning?

14. What was the last major battle that took place in the north?

15. Where did the last major battle of the Revolutionary War take place?

16. Where did the first battles between the British and the colonists take place?

Answers – Chapter 7

Battles of the Revolutionary War

1. Lexington

2. It's where the Revolutionary War started. It is known as "the shot heard 'round the world.'

3. Boston

4. William Prescott

5. The British

The Americans eventually ran out of ammunition and had to retreat.

6. Long Island, New York

7. Battle of Saratoga

8. Battle of Saratoga

9. France

10. Debt

11. Charleston

12. True

* *It prevented the British Navy from evacuating General Cornwallis and his troops at Yorktown. At this time, the French took over the control of the seas which was a decisive factor in the Siege of Yorktown which secured independence for the colonists.*

13. Battle of Trenton

14. The Battle of Monmouth

15. Yorktown

16. Lexington & Concord

8

FIGHTING FOR INDEPENDENCE

Answers are given at the end of the chapter.

1. How long did the American Revolutionary War last?

2. In what way was the Revolutionary War a civil war?

3. What salary did George Washington receive during the war?

4. What problems did George Washington face as Commander-in-Chief?

5. Who led Vermont's Green Mountain Boys?

6. What was Henry Knox's occupation before the war?

7. **True or False.** The Americans controlled Lake Champlain a strategically vital invasion route between the colonies and Canada when Benedict Arnold captured Fort Ticonderoga.

8. In the eighteenth century when wars were fought, what was common for the troops to do during the winter?

9. Where did General Washington make winter camp for his army?

10. **True or False.** Most men, from both armies, died in battle than from anything else.

11. Why were the smallpox inoculations given to Washington's troops done so in secrecy?

12. Other than smallpox, what other disease did the army troops suffer from?

13. In winter quarters, what was Baron von Steuben's, a newcomer from the Prussian army, role?

14. Who was General Washington's best infantry commander?

15. General Washington's artillery commander had been a bookseller in the days before the war and was knowledgeable about the military from books he read. Who was he?

16. What supplies were Washington's troops in need of?

17. In 1777, Washington was in desperate need of additional troops. What was offered as incentive for those who enlisted for three years or for the duration of the war?

18. Approximately how many men served in the Continental army throughout the war?

19. How did Washington fight the battle of smallpox amongst his troops?

20. **True or False.** The Continental army relied on information received from spies and local informants.

21. If a spy was caught, what was their sentence?

22. Benjamin Tallmadge put together a group of trustworthy men and women who gathered intelligence and passed it on to Washington achieving more than any other spies during the war. What was this group called?

23. Benedict Arnold had been one of the Continental army's most effective commanders. Why did he become a traitor?

24. What happened to Benedict Arnold when it was discovered he was a spy?

25. Washington feared losing his troops as their time was about to run out in which they had signed up for. As incentive he offered $10 bounty to stay on for an additional six weeks. Who risked their own finances to fund this bounty?

26. **True or False.** Always an insufficient amount of men in the Continental army, as the war continued some recruits would come from the British and Hessian prisoners of war.

Answers – Chapter 8

Fighting For Independence

1. 8 years

2. About one out of five of the colonists were Loyalists, or loyal to the king, and were against American independence. They didn't actually fight against each other, with few exceptions, but it caused strains among family, friends, and neighbors.

3. He didn't accept a salary. He asked only that his expenses would be covered.

4. *Any of the answers below would be correct.*

a) Most men were militia and not well trained.

b) Men would leave to tend to their farms.

c) Short on ammunition and weapons

d) Feeding and clothing the men

5. Ethan Allen

6. Bookstore owner

7. False

Fort Ticonderoga was captured by Ethan Allen and the Green Mountain Boys. Benedict Arnold had been commissioned to capture the fort, and rushed to Ethan Allen's camp when he learned of Allen's plans to capture the fort. Headstrong Allen took control, but "allowed" Arnold to accompany them as a volunteer.

8. The troops would withdraw to winter quarters.

It was hard for troops to find and replenish supplies and to move the troops during the winter, so it was common to camp through the winter months.

9. Valley Forge

10. False

More men died of disease; whether from a poor diet, insufficient shelter or clothing, or sanitation problems.

11. The soldiers who had been inoculated would be laid up, or incapacitated, for weeks afterward. If the British learned of this they could take advantage and attack during this time.

12. Typhus

13. His job was to drill the men, train them to fight with a bayonet, and to fire in unison.

This was of utmost importance, as when you had to move large groups of men quickly and to fight they had to move with precision. So even if he was a self-appointed Baron, his drills were of the utmost importance and he was an asset to the army.

14. Benedict Arnold

15. Henry Knox

16. You name it! They needed clothing, blankets, shoes, hats, shelter, food, water, ammunition.

17. They were offered $20 and the promise of 100 acres of land.

18. Approximately 100,000 men

* *This was 1/3 – ½ of the men of the United States. As many as ¼ would die before the end of the war.*

19. Forced inoculations

* *Martha Washington herself had to be inoculated before traveling to join her husband and the troops at Valley Forge.*

20. True

* *Nathan Hale along with local colonists who heard or saw information would then pass it on. The Culper Spy Ring and even women and children would help the cause by passing any information they had learned which would help the Continental army along to Washington.*

21. They were hanged.

22. The Culper Spy Ring

23. He felt he hadn't received the recognition and reward he felt he was due. While recovering from a wound he was recuperating in Philadelphia where he met and married a young girl who was a loyalist. She was a partner in her husband's treason. Arnold himself contacted the British and began providing them with intelligence.

24. He fled to the British.

He became a brigadier general and one of his first acts as a British soldier was to lead a raid against those he previously fought with. So, not only did he give strategic information to the British, but actually fought with them.

25. Robert Morris

26. True

They could earn their citizenship by fighting with the Continental army.

9

THE BRITISH

Answers are given at the end of the chapter.

1. What were the muskets of the British troops called?

2. Where did the British keep their prisoners of war?

3. The British also used spies. Who was the most famous traitor that passed information to the British army?

4. Many loyalists actually fought with the British. There were as many as 20%, or one in five, loyalists living among their patriot neighbors. What happened to the loyalists at the end of the war?

5. The British hired foreign mercenaries to fight the colonists. Who were they?

6. Name one of the British generals that fought in the Revolutionary War.

7. Who did the British try to get to aid them in their fight from the colonies?

8. Where was General Howe's base of operations?

9. Who replaced Sir William Howe?

Answers – Chapter 9

The British

1. Brown Bess

They were issued by Queen Elizabeth I is where they came up with the name Bess and the barrels were browned.

2. Most were kept on prison ships.

* *Over 47% of American prisoners died in captivity from overcrowded holds that were filthy and from a lack of sufficient food. In these conditions the men were weak and disease was a major problem.*

3. Benedict Arnold

4. They either moved to Canada or left with the British and went back to England losing their land and their fortunes.

5. Hessians who were German.

6. *Any of the names below would be correct.*

General Howe, Henry Clinton, John Burgoyne, Thomas Gage, Charles Cornwallis

7. Native Americans or loyalists; either would be correct.

8. Staten Island

9. Sir Henry Clinton

10

PEOPLE OF THE REVOLUTION

Answers are given at the end of the chapter.

1. Who rode into the countryside giving warning of the British movements to prepare the minutemen?

2. Paul Revere was to ride to Lexington to warn what two men that British troops were coming to arrest them?

3. Paul Revere's signal was meant to warn the patriots if the British were approaching by land or by sea by having a friend place the correct lanterns in the bell tower of the Christ Church (known today as the Old North Church). *Finish this stanza:*
     _____ if by land,
     _____ if by sea.

4. How were children, or young teens, involved in the Revolutionary War?

5. What young girl, at only sixteen years of age, took a ride similar to that of Paul Revere and William Dawes?

6. What future president signed up to fight in the Continental army at the age of thirteen?

7. Which of our future presidents were involved in the Revolutionary War?

8. Who was the U.S. Navy hero during the Revolutionary War?

9. What title has been attributed to John Paul Jones in honor of his courage?

10. What part did Martha Washington have in the Revolutionary War?

11. Whether fact or fiction, this woman is thought of as the one who sewed the nation's first flag. Who was she?

12. What woman was a folk hero, a patriot who carried pitchers of water to the soldiers during the Battle of Monmouth?

13. Name the woman who disguised herself as a man so she could serve in the Continental army.

14. What well-known black woman, as a supporter of the patriot cause, wrote a poem praising General Washington as Commander-in-Chief of the Continental army?

15. What is a camp follower? Who were they?

16. What twenty year old French aristocrat came to the colonies to offer his services to help fight for the American cause?

17. Major Henry Lee, Jr., also known as 'Light-Horse Harry,' had a son who would become even more famous than he was during the Civil War. Who was his son?

Answers – Chapter 10

People of the Revolution

1. Paul Revere and William Dawes

2. Sam Adams and John Hancock

3. One if by land, two if by sea

4. *Any of the answers below are correct.*

a) Play the drums or fife for the army

b) Taken to winter camps with their mother and father to do chores around the camp

c) Teenagers could fight with the army

d) Spy

5. Sybil Ludington

* Her father was a commander of the militia who was away with his militia when a message was delivered to their home warning that the British had found ammunition stores in Danbury, Connecticut. His sixteen year old daughter, realizing the importance of getting the message to him, rode forty miles through

the night, even fighting off a man with her father's musket along the way. Unfortunately, her message arrived too late as the British had raided the munitions storage and looted and burned the town. She would later receive thanks from General Washington for her brave act.

6. Andrew Jackson

* He was taken as a prisoner of war and wounded by a British officer when he refused to clean his boots.

7. **George Washington** as Commander-in-Chief. **John Adams** was not in the army, but was involved through Congress and a semi-participant in a naval engagement between a U.S. and British ship. **Thomas Jefferson** did not see action, but was Commander of Albemarlee County, militia at the start of the war. **James Madison** was a colonel in Virginia militia, but did not see any action. **James Monroe** was a major who was wounded at the Battle of Trenton. **John Quincy Adams** witnessed as a youth with his mother the Battle of Bunker Hill on a hillside near his home. He was with his father on the U.S. ship in a naval battle. **Andrew Jackson** was thirteen years old when he became a prisoner of war.

8. John Paul Jones

9. Father of the United States Navy

10. *Any answer below is correct.*

a) Called on women in the colonies for supplies and monetary donations for soldiers clothing and needs

b) Boosted morale and helped encourage both her husband and the soldiers at winter camp at Valley Forge.

c) Sewed socks and clothing for soldiers, nursed the sick and dying.

d) Donated $20,000 of her own money for clothing and supplies for the soldiers.

11. Betsy Ross

It is believed, but not proven and scoffed at by many historians, that Betsy Ross was visited by George Washington, George Ross, and Robert Morris in June of 1776, requesting her to sew the nation's flag. Whether fact or fiction, it was taught in history books in schools for over two hundred years.

12. Molly Pitcher

Molly Pitcher was a nickname for Mary Ludwig. She was a camp follower, a hard worker, who brought pitchers of water from a nearby spring for the soldiers to drink and to pour over the cannons to cool them down. When her husband collapsed during battle she took over his cannon and fought alongside the other soldiers.

13. Deborah Sampson

She was the first known woman to impersonate a man so she could fight for the cause. She was wounded in a battle and while being treated by a physician he discovered her true identity. It ended her military career, but she was honorably discharged.

14. Phillis Wheatley

15. Women and children who provided a service who followed the army. They had to pull their weight as supplies were low enough.

They were involved in nursing the wounded, sewing, laundry, and other duties.

16. Marquis de Lafayette

17. Robert E. Lee

11

THE END OF THE WAR

Answers are given at the end of the chapter.

1. Where did the surrender of the British take place?

2. What was the United States largest problem at the end of the war?

3. In what way, although not by choice, did the loyalists contribute to helping pay for the war?

4. What happened to the loyalists at the end of the war?

5. Where did Washington and his officers meet to have a farewell meal before he headed back to Mount Vernon at the end of the war?

6. In what year was America's independence recognized?

7. How long did the Revolutionary War last?

Answers – Chapter 11

The End Of The War

1. Yorktown

2. Debt

3. Their property was confiscated.

4. Many of the loyalists left with the British troops to go back to England while others went to Canada and still others remained in the United States. The ones that stayed couldn't hold office and were forced to pay punitive taxes. They were exiled in some states.

5. Fraunces Tavern in New York

* *Samuel Fraunces, the owner of the tavern, had aided the American cause during the war by passing on information he heard from the British while they were in his tavern.*

6. 1783

7.The Revolutionary War went on from 1775 – 1783, approximately 8 years.

12

CONSTITUTIONAL CONVENTION

Answers are given at the end of the chapter.

1. The Constitutional Convention was closed to the public so they wouldn't be pressured in any way and have their work compromised. Who kept records and notes of what was said and accomplished during these meetings?

2. What three men wrote 'The Federalist,' a collection of papers to defend the Constitution?

3. What were supporters of the Constitution called?

4. Name one person who was opposed to the new Constitution or who was an Anti-Federalist from these meetings.

5. Where did Congress choose to be the national capital?

6. What year was the Constitution ratified?

7. What were opponents of the Constitution called?

8. The Constitutional Convention met May of 1787. Twenty-one of

the men had fought in the war, eight had signed the Declaration of Independence, many had served in Congress, some had been governors. They were men with experience regardless of the fact that their average age was forty-two. Who was elected president of the Convention?

Answers – Chapter 12

Constitutional Convention

1. James Madison

2. Alexander Hamilton, James Madison, and John Jay

3. Federalists

4. *Any of the answers below are correct.*

a) Richard Henry Lee

b) Sam Adams

c) Patrick Henry

d) George Mason

e) George Clinton

5. New York

6. 1789

7. Anti-Federalists

8. George Washington

13

A NEW GOVERNMENT

Answers are given at the end of the chapter.

1. Who was elected the first president of the United States and who was elected the first vice-president?

2. Where was the first President of the United States sworn into office?

3. Who swore Washington into office?

4. How long was the term of the president?

5. Who was Washington's Secretary of State?

6. Who was the first Secretary of the Treasury?

7. Who was the first Secretary of War?

8. Who was the first Attorney General of the U.S.?

9. How many years was George Washington president?

10. Where was the nation's 2nd capital once it was moved from New York?

Answers – Chapter 13

A New Government

1. George Washington was president and John Adams was the vice president.

2. Federal Hall, New York City

3. Chancellor of New York Robert Livingston

4. 4 years

5. Thomas Jefferson

6. Alexander Hamilton

7. Henry Knox

8. Edmund Randolph

9. 8 years

10. Philadelphia

14

QUOTES OF THE PATRIOTS

Answers are given at the end of the chapter.

1. "We hold these truths to be self-evident: that all men are created equal."

2. When Congress met to decide if the colonies would fight for their independence, who said: "We must hang together, or, most assuredly, we shall all hang separately"?

3. When Congress met on the issue of independence, who said: "The question was not whether, by a declaration of independence, we should make ourselves what we are not; but whether we should declare a fact which already exists"?

4. What member of Congress wrote this to his wife: "The second day of July, 1776; will be the most memorable epochs in the history of America..."?

5. "There! I guess King George will be able to read that without his spectacles."

6. "There is a certain enthusiasm in liberty, that makes human nature rise above itself, in acts of bravery and heroism."

7. "I have not yet begun to fight."

8. "The Constitution shall never be construed...to prevent the people of the United States who are peaceable citizens from keeping their own arms."

9. "Give me liberty or give me death!"

10. "One if by land, two if by sea."

11. "To be prepared for war is one of the most effective means of preserving peace."

12. "Don't shoot until you see the whites of their eyes."

13. "I only regret that I have but one life to lose for my country."

14. "It's not tyranny we desire; it's a just, limited federal government."

15. "In this world nothing is certain but death and taxes."

Answers – Chapter 14

Quotes of the Patriots

1. Thomas Jefferson

2. Benjamin Franklin

3. Thomas Jefferson

4. John Adams

He was right; only the day America celebrated would not be the 2nd of July, but the 4th of July.

5. John Hancock

6. Alexander Hamilton

7. John Paul Jones

8. Samuel Adams

9. Patrick Henry

10. Paul Revere

11. George Washington

12. William Prescott

13. Nathan Hale

14. Alexander Hamilton

15. Ben Franklin

He was referring to the Constitution, and the full quote was, "Our Constitution is in actual operation; everything appears to promise that it will last; but in this world nothing is certain but death and taxes."

www.ingramcontent.com/pod-product-compliance
Lightning Source LLC
Chambersburg PA
CBHW060037050426
42448CB00012B/3045